Cowgirl Amy
At the
Cow Kid Zoo

*A*dvantage
BOOKS

Dr. Psalm

The Adventures of Cowgirl Amy!
Cowgirl Amy at the Cow Kid Zoo by Dr Psalm
Copyright © 2014 by Peace Psalm LLC
All Rights Reserved.
ISBN: 978-1-59755-255-4

Published by: ADVANTAGE BOOKS™
    Longwood, Florida USA
    www.advbookstore.com

First Printing: September 2014
14 15 16 17 18 19 20 10 9 8 7 6 5 4 3 2 1
Printed in the United States of America

Cowgirl Amy at the Cow Kid Zoo

"Halo and Howdy! My name is Cowgirl Amy! I love God, my family, friends, and my pony Slow Poke!

My Grandma Linda and I go on secret missions. We find God and praise in the most amazing places. Come and join us!

Today Grandma Linda is calling me for a secret mission at the Cow Kid Zoo. She wears her green cowgirl hat when she has an exciting mission for me!

Grandma Linda called me today on Skype. She was wearing her green hat, so I knew she had a fun secret mission for me!

"Halo my Cowgirl Amy! How are you? I have a secret mission adventure for my Cowgirl Amy!" said Grandma. "It will take place at the Cow Kid Zoo! I have hidden clues for you in scroll tubes that spell out a Bible book and verses!" said Grandma Linda.

"All right and Yee Haw! Let's get started!" I said.

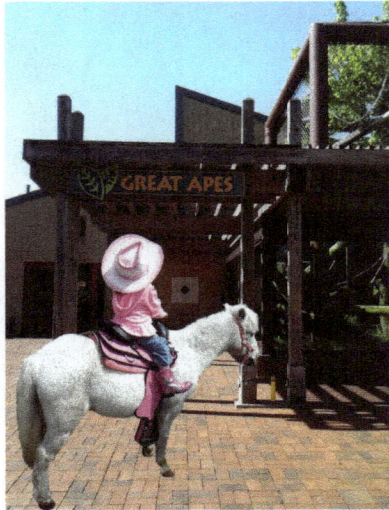

Grandma Linda said, "The first letter of the animal name is 'G'. You will find a scroll tube with the letter for the next animal when you find our 'G' animal. I have a hint. It is a primate, and your great aunt Suzanne works with them!" She asked, "Do you know what it is?"

I said, "I know! It is a gorilla!"

"Exactly Cowgirl Amy! Be sure to say hello to your great aunt Suzanne when you stop there." said Grandma Linda.

"Yee haw! I absolutely will say halo, hello and howdy to her! She is very nice." I giggled. "I found the scroll tube Grandma Linda! It is next to the pillar!" I said.

Grandma Linda said "Awesome! Let's pray!"

GORILLA

Thank you Jesus for gorillas, so big and strong.

They call out to each other with a cheerful song.

In the name of Jesus we pray, Amen!

"Let's keep track of our Bible book! G_____" with a smile.

Grandma Linda asked, "What did you find inside the scroll tube?" I said, "I found the letter E." Grandma Linda said "Good! I have a hint for you! The mammal is very large." She asked, "Do you know what it is?"

I said "I know! It is an elephant!" "Awesome Cowgirl Amy!

You are right!" said Grandma Linda.

'Ha! I see the next scroll tube! It is on top of the elephant's head!' I said.

"Excellent find Cowgirl Amy! Let's pray" said Grandma Linda.

ELEPHANT

Thank you Lord for elephants big and small. They reach with their trunks to eat a great haul.

In the name of Jesus we pray, Amen!

Hi friends, let's keep track of our Bible book! GE_____

Grandma Linda asked "What did you find in the scroll tube?"

I said "I found the letter 'N'. That is a hard one Grandma Linda."

Smiling at me, Grandma Linda said "I have a hint for you! The amphibian is small." She asked, "Do you know what it is now?"

I said, "I know! It is a newt!"

"Awesome Cowgirl Amy! You are correct!" said Grandma Linda.

'Wow! Oh how fun! The next scroll tube is right in front of the building! I almost lost my boot stopping Slow Poke in time!" I said laughing.

"Another great find Cowgirl Amy! Let's pray," said Grandma Linda.

NEWTS

Thank you God for Newts, in water and on land. They are quick to move and make quite a stand.

In the name of Jesus we pray, Amen!

Let's keep track of our Bible book! GEN_____

Grandma Linda asked, "What did you find in the scroll tube?"

I said, "I found the letter E."

Grandma Linda said "Good! I have a hint for you! The bird is a national symbol." She asked, "Do you know what it is?"

I said, "I know! It is an eagle!" "Awesome Cowgirl Amy! You are right again!" said Grandma Linda.

"Let's pray" said Grandma Linda.

EAGLE

Thank you Lord for the eagles so bold and strong. They are the symbol of America that loves you as Lord.

In the name of Jesus we pray, Amen!

Let's keep track of our Bible book! GENE___

Grandma Linda asked "What did you find in the scroll tube this time?"

I said, "I found the letter 'S'."

Grandma Linda said "Good! I have a hint for you! It is a bird with long legs. She asked, "Do you know what it is?"

I said "I know! It is a stork!"

"Excellent Cowgirl Amy! You are correct!" said Grandma Linda.

"Hey! I see the next scroll canister over there! It is behind the viewer for the storks and other animals!" I said.

"Well done Cowgirl Amy! Let's pray" said Grandma Linda.

STORK

Dear Jesus, thank you for the stork with legs so tall.

It is so pretty, and I like the way it wades in the water with reeds and all.

Through Jesus we pray, Amen!

Let's keep track of our Bible book! GENES__

Grandma Linda asked, "Which letter did you find this time?"

I said, "I found the letter 'I'."

Grandma Linda said "Good! I have a hint for you! It is a mammal that runs very quickly." She asked, "Do you know what it is?"

I said, "I know! It is an impala!"

"Excellent Cowgirl Amy! You are correct!" said Grandma Linda.

"Let's pray," said Grandma Linda.

IMPALA

Dear Jesus, Thank you for the impala so quiet and quick.

They run so gracefully, and jump so high lickety-split.

In the name of Jesus we pray, Amen!

Let's keep track of our Bible book! GENESI_

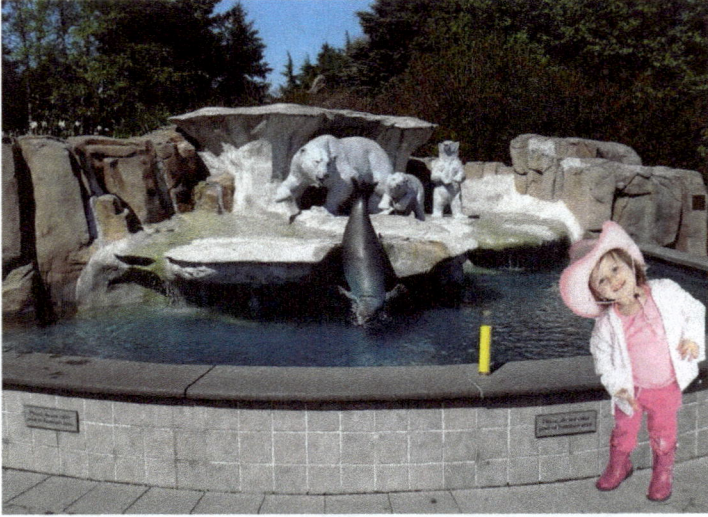

Grandma Linda asked, "This is the last letter. What did you find in the scroll box?"

I said, "I found the letter 'S'."

Grandma Linda said "Wonderful! I have a hint for you! It is a mammal that swims." She asked, "Do you know what it is?"

I said, "I know! It is a seal!"

"Exactly Cowgirl Amy! You are correct again!" said Grandma Linda.

"This is fun! Hey friends, do you see the scroll tube between the seal and me?" I asked.

"Very good Cowgirl Amy! You are very good at solving the clues and finding the scroll tubes! Let's pray" said Grandma Linda.

SEAL

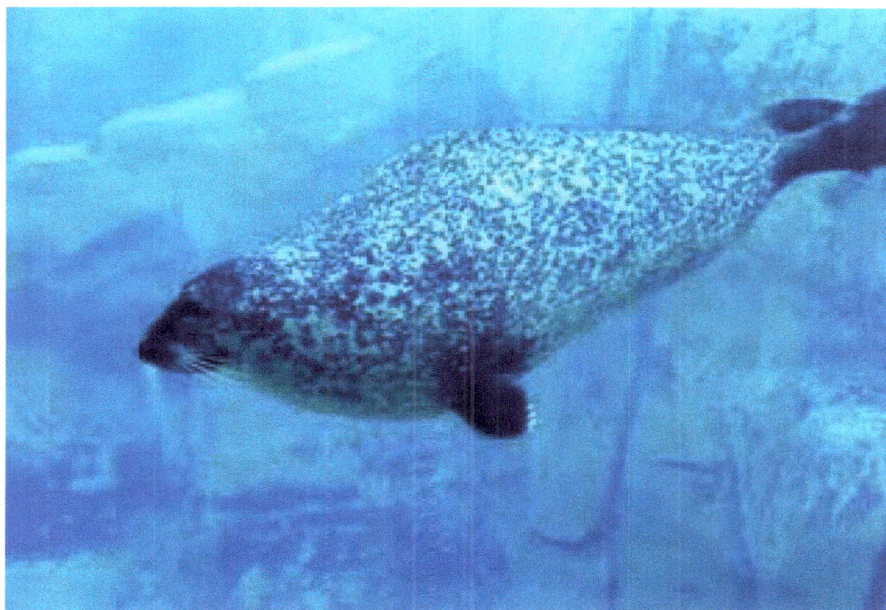

Dear Lord, Thank you for the seal on land and in water.

They swim so nicely with fins and wiggles.

In the name of Jesus we pray, Amen!

"Now we have all of the letters of the book!" said Grandma Linda.

"It is GENESIS!" I said.

"You are right!" said Grandma Linda.

Grandma Linda asked, "The last message is a number. What did you find in the scroll tube?"

I said "I found the numbers 6:1 – 9:17."

Grandma Linda said "Wonderful!" Then she asked me with a smile "Do you know what it is?"

I said, "I know! It is the story of Noah's Ark!"

"Right again Cowgirl Amy! It is a great story for your mom and dad to read to you!" said Grandma Linda.

"Let's pray" said Grandma Linda.

Dear Lord, thank you for the animals in Noah's Ark. Thank you for Cow Kid Zoo that shares them in their park.

In the name of Jesus we pray, Amen!

Adios for now my friends! I am going home now. I will ask my mom and dad to read the story of Noah's Ark to me tonight at bedtime!

Join us next time when Grandma Linda and I go on a secret mission to find a new Christmas holiday family tradition!

Until we meet again! Your friend, Cowgirl Amy

Dear Lord, thank you for my friends and your wonderful animals. Please watch over them and shower them with your love.

In the name of Jesus we pray, Amen!

Join Cowgirl Amy this year in her adventures!

Cowgirl Amy and the Prayer Garden: A Flower a Day

Cowgirl Amy and the Easter Adventure – A Tradition Begins

Cowgirl Amy and Favorite Prayers for Mom

Cowgirl Amy and Favorite Prayers for Dad

Cowgirl Amy and the Adventure at the Cow Kid Zoo

Cowgirl Amy and the Christmas Celebration – A Tradition Begins

Prayers, blessing and cheer!

Special Thanks and Recognition

Toledo Zoo/Casey Cook: For the pictures of all of the animals, and the pre-altered photos on the front and back covers of this book.

SUPPORT YOUR LOCAL ZOO!

For more information contact:

Dr Psalm
C/O Advantage Books
P.O. Box 160847
Altamonte Springs, FL 32716
info@ advbooks.com

To purchase additional copies of this book or other books published by
Advantage Books call our order number at: 407-788-3110 (Book
Orders Only)

or visit our bookstore website at: www.advbookstore.com

*A*dvantage
BOOKS

Longwood, Florida, USA
"we bring dreams to life"™
www.advbooks.com